Erosion

by Becky Olien

Consultant:
Francesca Pozzi, Research Associate
Center for International Earth Science Information Network
Columbia University

Bridgestone Books
an imprint of Capstone Press
Mankato, Minnesota

Bridgestone Books are published by Capstone Press
151 Good Counsel Drive, P.O. Box 669, Mankato, Minnesota 56002
http://www.capstone-press.com

Library of Congress Cataloging-in-Publication Data
Olien, Rebecca.
    Erosion/by Becky Olien.
    p. cm.—(The Bridgestone science library)
    Includes bibliographical references and index.
    ISBN 0-7368-0950-3
    1. Erosion—Juvenile literature. [1. Erosion.] I. Title. II. Series.
QE571 .O46 2002
551.3'02—dc21   00-012592

Summary: Discusses water, wind, ice, and soil erosion.

Editorial Credits
Rebecca Glaser, editor; Karen Risch, product planning editor; Linda Clavel, designer and
    illustrator; Jeff Anderson and Deirdre Barton, photo researchers

Photo Credits
International Stock/Bob Firth, cover, 1
Digital Wisdom, globe image
Ernesto Burciaga/Photo Agora, 6
John Elk III, 10, 18
Kent and Donna Dannen, 4, 14
Kevin Vandivier/The Viesti Collection, Inc., 16
Photo Network/Bill Terry, 12
Robert Maust/Photo Agora, 8
Robert McCaw, 20

Cover Photo: Soil erosion near Mount Rainier, Washington
**The author thanks Jane Anklam, soil conservationist, for information and help while writing
this book.**

2 3 4 5 6 07 06 05 04 03 02

Table of Contents

What Is Erosion?

Erosion changes Earth's surface. Water, wind, and ice cause erosion. These powerful forces in nature break rock and soil into smaller pieces. Water, wind, and ice carry pebbles and grains of sand from place to place.

Most changes caused by erosion take millions of years. Erosion carves away rock and creates valleys, caves, and canyons. Erosion wears away the sides and tops of mountain peaks. The Appalachian Mountains once were as tall as the Rocky Mountains. The Appalachian Mountains are now 15,000 feet (4,600 meters) shorter because of erosion.

People can change the land and cause erosion to happen faster. Erosion is harmful when it happens too quickly. People cut down forests to make new homes, businesses, or farmland. Trees help protect soil from erosion. Soil erodes faster without the trees to keep soil in place.

Erosion has worn down the Appalachian Mountains.

Wind Erosion

Wind erodes the surface of Earth. Wind moves small grains of sand and soil. Only the smallest pieces of rock are light enough to be picked up by the wind. These pieces of rock then wear against large rocks and the sides of mountains.

Wind erosion has the greatest effect in deserts. Desert soil is mostly sand. Wind easily blows the sand. In some deserts, the wind pushes sand into large hills called dunes. In the Sahara Desert in Africa, dunes can be 1,000 feet (305 meters) tall.

Sand carried in the wind scrapes against rock and wears it into shapes. Wind erosion can create natural arches of rock. Arches National Park in eastern Utah has many of these formations.

Wind erodes land that is not protected by plants and trees. Fire, floods, volcanoes, and people remove plants from the soil. Wind then blows away the top layer of soil. Without topsoil, farmers cannot grow crops well.

Wind erosion can create natural arches of rock. This arch is in Arches National Park in Utah.

Water Erosion

Water has more power to erode than wind does. Flowing water removes soil, pebbles, and small rocks. Acid in rain contributes to erosion because it makes cracks and holes in rock. Rain and snow wash broken rock down slopes to rivers. Rivers carry rocks downstream. The rocks move sand along the river bottoms. Sand and small rocks mix with water. The water carries this sediment to oceans.

Rivers can erode rocks. Over millions of years, rivers wear away rock to make canyons and other rock formations. Fast-flowing water wears away river banks where rivers turn. After millions of years, rock erodes under the curves, leaving arches of rock. The arches look like bridges.

Waves also cause erosion. Lake and ocean waves pound against rocky shores and wear them away.

Waves have eroded this rocky shore along Lake Huron.

Fun Fact

A glacier carried boulders 500 miles (800 kilometers) from Norway to England.

Ice Erosion

Ice erosion is the strongest type of erosion. In winter, water between rocks freezes. Ice takes up more space than water. The ice pushes on the rocks and cracks them. Over time, ice breaks apart rocks.

Glaciers are large sheets of pressed snow and ice. Their heavy weight makes them creep forward. Most glaciers move only a few inches each day. Rocks freeze to the underside of the ice. The rocks in the ice scrape the surface of the land as the glacier moves.

Glaciers leave behind small rocks, soil, and water when they melt. Pieces of ice break off and melt into lakes. The Great Lakes in the United States and Canada were made by glaciers. They are some of the biggest lakes in the world.

Millions of years ago, glaciers covered one-third of Earth. In some areas, the ice was 1 mile (1.6 kilometers) thick. Today, glaciers are near the north and south poles and on the highest mountains.

Paradise Glacier in Washington erodes Mount Rainier a little bit each year.

Fun Fact

Wind, water, and ice erosion carve the Grand Canyon slightly wider and deeper each year.

The Grand Canyon

The Grand Canyon is in the southwestern United States. It is 277 miles (446 kilometers) long and 1 mile (1.6 kilometers) deep.

About 2 billion years ago, oceans covered the Grand Canyon. The oceans deposited sediments in layers. The oldest rock layer is at the bottom of the canyon. The top layer is about 240 million years old.

The Colorado River started flowing about 20 million years ago. It carved into the Grand Canyon. About 17 million years ago, plates in Earth's crust lifted up layers of rock. The Colorado River stayed at the bottom and cut deeper into the canyon.

The uplift stopped about 5 million years ago. The Colorado River, rain, and ice continue to erode the canyon. Rain loosens rock along the river. The river carries loose rock and sediment that scrapes against the walls of the Grand Canyon. Water also seeps into cracks in the rocks and freezes. The ice breaks the rocks and widens the cracks.

The flowing water of the Colorado River is one force that erodes the Grand Canyon.

Fun Fact

More water lies underground
than in all the lakes and
rivers above ground.

Erosion Underground

Erosion also happens underground. Rain soaks into soil. The water slowly seeps through layers of rock and becomes groundwater. The water can pick up minerals and carbon dioxide as it passes through the rock. These elements make the water acidic. The acid in the water erodes other rocks.

Water easily can erode limestone. The calcium in bones and shells from dead animals forms limestone. Acid in water dissolves the calcium in limestone and breaks the rock. Acid in water sometimes dissolves underground limestone and creates caves.

Mammoth Cave in Kentucky is the longest cave in the world. It was formed by the erosion of underground limestone. Mammoth Cave has more than 300 miles (483 kilometers) of connecting tunnels and underground rooms. Water eroded the cave in stages over millions of years.

Water erosion underground made this formation in Mammoth Cave.

Hurricanes

Hurricanes have strong winds that cause erosion. A hurricane is a storm that begins above warm ocean water. The air spins and picks up moisture and heat from the ocean. The heat gives energy to the storm and helps increase the wind speed.

Hurricanes can destroy land and cities. In 1992, the winds of Hurricane Andrew blew 141 miles (227 kilometers) per hour. These winds destroyed houses and trees along Florida's and Louisiana's coastlines.

Tidal surges are huge waves that crash onto a shore. Tidal surges break buildings, cause flooding, and erode coastal soil during hurricanes. In 1996, Hurricane Fran's tidal surge was more than 16 feet (4.9 meters) tall. It crashed into North Carolina's coast and caused heavy flooding. The flooding eroded much of the coastal soil.

Heavy rains sometimes follow hurricanes and cause floods. Floods erode soil and can sweep away buildings.

The strong winds of hurricanes can erode land.

Soil Erosion

Plants grow in topsoil. For this reason, topsoil is the most valuable part of soil. A mixture of rotting plants and animals, water, air, and crushed rock makes up topsoil. Topsoil is rich in nutrients that plants need to grow. It takes hundreds of years for 1 inch (2.5 centimeters) of topsoil to form. Few plants can grow where topsoil has eroded.

Erosion destroys and moves topsoil. Wind blows dry topsoil across open fields and prairies. Heavy rains wash away loose topsoil into rivers. Rivers then carry topsoil to the oceans.

Millions of acres of soil were eroded during the Dust Bowl of the 1930s. Farmers in the Great Plains plowed soil to grow crops. The soil was dry. Wind lifted clouds of soil into the air as dust. In 1935, winds made a cloud of dust 2 miles (3.2 kilometers) wide. As much as 3 feet (1 meter) of topsoil was lost in some places during the Dust Bowl.

Strong winds can pick up soil and create dust storms like this one in Morocco. Morocco is a country in Africa.

What Is a Soil Conservationist?

Soil conservationists help land owners protect their soil from erosion. They help farmers find ways to save topsoil. They give city builders ideas to keep soil in place during construction. Soil conservationists plant trees and find other ways to fix areas where erosion is ruining the land. Slowing erosion also prevents fertilizers that farmers use from washing into rivers and polluting water. A soil conservationist helps many people use land wisely.

Conserving the Land

Conservation is protecting land. People can help conserve land by protecting natural areas from erosion. Forests soak up water and hold soil in place. Wetlands hold in water to help prevent floods that wash away soil.

Planting in new areas also protects land. People can plant trees and plants on slopes and along rivers. The plants' roots hold together soil and help protect the soil from erosion. Trees and plants in flat, dry places protect the soil from wind erosion. Farmers plant rows of trees between fields. The trees act as a windbreak.

People also can help conserve land by controlling air pollution. Air pollution mixes with the water in clouds and falls as acid rain. Acid rain speeds up erosion by dissolving rock. Acid rain also kills plants that protect soil.

Conservation helps protect soil and land from erosion. Soil cannot easily be replaced.

Trees planted in a row on open land make a windbreak. Windbreaks can help prevent soil erosion.

Hands On: Make a Sugar Cave

Water and wind erode land. This erosion sometimes creates caves. You can learn how water and wind form caves.

What You Need

2 cups sugar
1/4 cup water
Bowl
Spoon

Pie plate
Spray bottle full of water
Straw

What You Do

1. Mix 2 cups sugar and 1/4 cup water in a bowl.
2. Stir the mixture and place it on a pie plate.
3. Form the mixture into a mountain shape. Store it in the freezer overnight.
4. Place the pie plate in a sink.
5. Squirt the side of the sugar mountain to form a cave.
6. Blow through a straw at the cave opening you made in step 5.

A sugar mountain can be eroded like limestone can. Water dissolves the sugar like acid dissolves limestone. Your breath blowing through the straw is like wind. You make the cave with water and wind erosion.

Words to Know

acid (ASS-id)—a substance that pollutes water and erodes limestone

carbon dioxide (KAR-buhn dye-OK-side)—a gas found naturally in the air; carbon dioxide has no smell or color.

conservation (kon-sur-VAY-shuhn)—the protection of natural resources; conservation can protect soil from erosion.

dissolve (di-ZOLV)—to break into tiny pieces when mixed with water

glacier (GLAY-shur)—a large, slow-moving sheet of ice and snow

sediment (SED-uh-muhnt)—bits of rock and sand carried by water or wind

tidal surge (TYD-uhl SURJ)—a sudden, strong wave

windbreak (WIND-brayk)—a row of trees planted to block the wind and prevent soil erosion.

Read More

Downs, Sandra. *Shaping the Earth: Erosion.* Exploring Planet Earth. Brookfield, Conn.: Twenty-First Century Books, 2000.

Rutten, Joshua. *Erosion.* Chanhassen, Minn.: Child's World, 1999.

Winner, Cherie. *Erosion.* A Carolrhoda Earth Watch Book. Minneapolis: Carolrhoda Books, 1999.

Useful Addresses

Saskatchewan Soil
   Conservation Association
Box 1360
Indian Head, SK S0G 2K0
Canada

United States Geological
   Survey
345 Middlefield Road
Menlo Park, CA 94025

Internet Sites

Ask S.K. Worm about Soil
http://www.nhq.nrcs.usda.gov/CCS/squirm/skworm.html
The Geology of the Grand Canyon
http://www.kaibab.org/geology/gc_geol.htm
Park Geology Tour of National Parks
http://www.aqd.nps.gov/grd/tour

Index